LEISA ANSLINGER

# Here Comes Everybody!

*Whole*

*Community*

*Catechesis*

*in the*

*Parish*

## TWENTY-THIRD PUBLICATIONS

185 WILLOW STREET • PO BOX 180 • MYSTIC, CT 06355
TEL: 1-800-321-0411 • FAX: 1-800-572-0788
Bayard E-MAIL: ttpubs@aol.com • www.twentythirdpublications.com

# Here Comes Everybody!

## Whole Community Catechesis in the Parish

Second printing 2005

Twenty-Third Publications
A Division of Bayard
185 Willow Street
P.O. Box 180
Mystic, CT 06355
(860) 536-2611 or (800) 321-0411
www.twentythirdpublications.com

ISBN:1-58595-364-4
Library of Congress Catalog Card Number: 2004107490
Printed in the U.S.A.

# ACKNOWLEDGMENTS

My deepest gratitude must be expressed to Father Jan Kevin Schmidt and the people of Immaculate Heart of Mary Parish. It is a true privilege and joy to travel the path of discipleship in such a community. Your dedication to the gospel is inspiring.

"Thank you" seems a pale expression of gratefulness for friends and colleagues David Haas and the team of Music Ministry Alive!, Bill Huebsch, Dan Mulhall, Kay Hohner Stefanics, and Elizabeth Bookser Barkley. Your support, insight, and coaching has been indispensable, and your friendship more valued than words can express.

Thanks as well to Gwen Costello and everyone at Twenty-Third Publications for their enthusiastic support, and to Diane Lampitt and the staff at Harcourt Religion Publishers for their encouragement.

To Steve, Mike, and Carrie, whose love reminds me of God's love every moment of every day: I dedicate this book to you on this twenty-fifth anniversary of the beginning of our family, May 19, 2004.

Solo Dios basta.

# CONTENTS

# INTRODUCTION

Here comes everybody! Wouldn't it be great if you could say this about your parish faith formation gatherings? This is, of course, the long-term goal of whole community catechesis, and I can tell you from experience that once you embrace this process, people are changed and the parish is transformed. Even after seven years on this journey, the transformation still takes me by surprise. Yet whole community catechesis doesn't just happen on its own. It is the result of many things working together to build a community of disciples, where every person in the parish is invited to keep learning and growing in their faith.

Many elements must come together to form this kind of parish community. First and foremost, the Sunday celebration of the Eucharist has to be the focal point of all faith formation. (In my parish, a hundred or more parishioners are involved each week in liturgical ministries.) Homilies have to be well-prepared and resonate with people's experience. The gospel has to be proclaimed boldly, with no attempt to side-step difficult issues. Everybody in the community has to be challenged to embrace conversion as a way of life. All who are assembled have to be drawn into full participation, to experience Mass in a way that really leads them to think deeply about their relationship with Christ.

Whole community catechesis doesn't end with Sunday Mass, however. People need to be sent forth to love and serve the Lord and be given opportunities to do so, in addition to those provided by their daily lives in the family, at work, and so on. Ministries within the parish community have to extend beyond the local area to parts of the world that are most in need. In these ways parishioners come to understand that being a disciple calls one to selfless service.

"You know what I love about coming to these evenings?" a parishioner asked me recently as we greeted people arriving for a faith formation gathering. "It isn't just about deepening my faith, although I have to admit my life has changed much in the last few years, as I've grown closer to Christ and learned about prayer and so much more…. It's the people, too—seeing friends and meeting people I have seen at Mass but have never spoken to. Now I see people in my neighborhood, and we have something in common. My children feel like they're a part of something special. They believe they can make a difference in the world. I'm beginning to think they're right! When we live our faith so deeply, it's bound to change things around us."

This kind of ongoing formation, which is both profound and active, requires commitment on the part of the parish community as well as commitment from individuals. Catechesis-for-all invites people to celebrate the eucharistic liturgy and the sacraments fully, consciously, and actively. It leads them to an understanding that conversion is a lifelong endeavor, one that we all enter together. Catechesis-for-all is also the path that leads people to a deeper awareness of God's presence and to reflection on that presence throughout the week. Catechesis-for-all assures that every person in the parish has a foundation in the teachings of the church. Catechesis-for-all invites every household of faith to embrace a life of change, of transformation through the power of the Holy Spirit. Once people have experienced these things, they want to share this Good News through the way they live.

This is what is happening in my parish—really! It wasn't always this way, though. Just a few years ago, Immaculate Heart of Mary Parish was like many Catholic parishes. Parishioners dreamed of a different sort of experience, but the dream seemed distant and unrealistic. "What if…." they asked.

- "What if families with children who attend public schools didn't feel like second-class citizens?"

- "What if children in our parish school understood that 'mission' isn't a faraway place but, rather, a way of life?"

- "What if, instead of dropping children off at an evening class or for the sacramental preparation process, parents saw themselves as integral to their child's formation in faith?"

- "What if everyone in the parish recognized that their relationship with Christ calls them to a living discipleship, resulting in ongoing faith formation, service, and relationships with others—all centered on being eucharistic people?"

## A TIME OF TRANSITION

Seven years ago Immaculate Heart of Mary was a parish in the midst of a painful transition. The year before a new pastor, Father Jan Schmidt, had arrived. He found a community divided into many factions and with a large debt. The parishioners had been lulled into an awkward complacency, convinced that things could be better but not knowing where or how to begin.

By the spring of 1997, the Worship Commission, under the direction of Father Jan, had made adjustments in the way the Sunday Eucharist was celebrated. Parish leaders had met to discuss their concerns, and a long-range planning process was under way. Open meetings were held, and more people began to dream of the possibilities.

Within the long-range plan formulated in 1997, catechesis-for-all was one of the highest priorities. People voiced their hopes that the parish would become a welcoming place in which families could gather to learn about their faith, and in which children, youth, and adults could be drawn to service. The individuals with a similar belief system who had gathered at Immaculate Heart of Mary Parish were becoming a community of faith, envisioning a future together that would celebrate and value every member.

That spring, we made a commitment to whole community catechesis. Right from the start, the response of children, teens, and adults assured us that something wonderful was beginning. Our community has never looked back! Our 1400 elementary school children and 3060 families—over 10,000 people—are embracing discipleship as a way of life.

Leading people to full, conscious, and active participation in the liturgy, helping them to better understand Sacred Scripture, acquainting them with the church's theological and moral teaching, calling them to work for justice and peace, and giving them opportunities to serve one another and their needy brothers and sisters have all led to a vibrant, exciting, and all-consuming family of faith that truly embraces gospel living. Here are some of the positive signs.

• Our children's scores in the Assessment of Catechesis/ Religious Education (ACRE) have risen dramatically (chapter six includes a description of how ACRE has been used to demonstrate changes in understanding and lived faith over time).

• We have seen an increase in the number of parish-ioners who regularly attend Mass and of parishioners who serve in ministry to the parish, the local communi-ty, and our twin parish in Nicaragua.

• While not the largest parish in our archdiocese, Immaculate Heart of Mary contributes more than double that of any other parish toward mission and outreach. Our weekly Mass attendance is the largest of any parish in our archdiocese.

• Adult faith formation is now understood to be the norm, and parents routinely express their gratitude for the many opportunities to learn. No longer do they wonder why their parish isn't doing more for them. Now they understand that all of us have to work together to support each other's journey of faith.

• It's also now the norm that planning and implementation of catechesis be a total parish endeavor. In fact, the community clearly understands that it is both the agent and the subject of faith formation. Possibilities for processes constantly surface, and many will become reality through the generous service of community members. Those "what if…" questions are being answered. "What if" is giving way to the bright promise of more to come.

It seems that no matter where I go these days, people in catechetical circles are asking how to establish a broad array of faith formation opportunities like the ones I have just described. Catechetical leaders have read the *General Directory for Catechesis* and *Our Hearts Were Burning within Us*, along with a variety of other documents, all of which present a vision of church that is both exciting and challenging. The vision is this: that one day the church, all the people of God, will fully, consciously, and actively participate, not only in the celebration of the liturgy but in all aspects of parish life. In turn this life will lead them to a deeper relationship with Christ, who sends them forth to love and to serve others.

Many pastoral leaders are searching for resources to help them implement the principles of whole community catechesis. Where do we begin? What does this form of catechesis "look like"? Are there paths to implementing it that other parishes have already found to be beneficial? Are there mistakes we should avoid?

This book is written to be just such a resource. It reflects the experience of people who have been realizing the principles of whole community catechesis for some time now. *Here Comes Everybody!* will describe a variety of approaches to the implementation of whole community catechesis, and will also offer some practical advice. My hope in writing it is that you will find here the encouragement you need in order to step onto this path yourselves.

# CHAPTER ONE

# TOWARD
# DISCIPLESHIP

As you begin reading this guide to implementing whole community catechesis, take a few moments to think about what you most hope will take place in your parish. What needs to be changed, transformed, or adjusted so that everyone in your parish will begin or grow in their relationship with Christ? What is already in place that can be celebrated and built upon? What do your parish leaders think of when they hear the phrase "whole community catechesis" or "total parish catechesis"? Are they ready to hear: "Here comes everybody"?

The principles of whole community catechesis are simple,

yet when we approach faith formation using these principles, the transformation that takes place in individual lives and the life of the community is amazing.

A few weeks ago, as I was preparing for a workshop with catechetical leaders, I asked our Formation Advisory Commission members to summarize as succinctly as they could what has happened in our parish as a result of implementing the principles we will be exploring. (Later in this book I'll explain more about how commission members are invited and formed for this ministry.) I share their comments here as a way of encouraging you to dream boldly as you begin or continue on this path.

We have two teen commission members. During prayer at the beginning of one meeting, Molly, one of our teens, told us how much support she felt after the accidental death of a friend from a neighboring school. She explained that, while few in our parish knew the young man who had died, many persons had called, visited, and listened with compassion to those from our community who knew him.

Later in the meeting, as I asked for the commission's thoughts about what is taking place as a result of whole community catechesis, one member began by saying, "Molly not only knows what the church teaches, she is living it, and we are helping her to live it by believing in her and her peers. We help her see that her journey is as important as ours, that she is a full member of our community, and that she and her peers deserve our support."

Another continued, "I watched as our children rejoined us at the end of our gathering two weeks ago, and I said to myself, 'Finally, we're all together.' We understand that the community is best when we're all together. I was reminded of conversations we've had here about remembering that everyone is formed in the image and likeness of God, and I recognized the value of each person who was at the gathering that night."

A young man who was recently received into full communion in the church said, "I remember a saying from when I was growing up.

'It's better to be a sermon than to preach a sermon.' Here I meet lots of people who are living the sermon. Often they don't use words, but they sure do live the gospel." Another member then said, "I remember this parish before all of this began. It has been a gradual process, but I believe we have changed and grown in many ways. It's exciting to be a part of this." I left the meeting convinced once again that what has happened as a result of whole community catechesis needs to be shared.

"Were not our hearts burning within us while he was talking to us on the road, while he was opening the scriptures to us?" (Luke 24:32). Like the disciples on the road to Emmaus, we sometimes find the Christian journey perplexing. *Our Hearts Were Burning within Us, the U.S. Bishops' Pastoral Plan for Adult Faith Formation,* encourages us to walk side by side with people on the pathway of life. The bishops wrote:

> We will ask them questions and listen attentively as they speak of their joys, hopes, griefs, and anxieties. We will share with them the living word of God, which can touch their hearts and minds and unfold the deep meaning of their experience in the light of all that Jesus said and did. We will trust the capacity of prayer and sacrament to open their eyes to the presence and love of Christ. We will invite them to live and share this Good News in the world. This is the way for us to acknowledge the life-giving power and evangelizing dynamic of encountering Jesus today—just as the two disciples felt their hearts burn within them and returned in haste to Jerusalem to tell their story of meeting Jesus (#7-10).

Whole community catechesis creates such a path toward living discipleship. The journey for those who follow Christ is more fruitful when we travel together, learning and growing, sharing and supporting each other along the way. Before we get into the process itself, let's look at the dimensions that are the foundation of whole community catechesis. These eight dimensions are like markers along the path, helping us make our way, and keeping us focused as we invite people to a deep, transforming relationship with Christ. After describing each one, I will offer reflection and/or discussion questions you can share within your own parish.

## 1. The Eucharistic Liturgy Is Central

We are a sacramental people, and our prayer together forms us, especially the Sunday celebration of the Eucharist. So rich is the liturgy that a lifetime of celebrations cannot contain the mystery of Christ's love and what that love calls us to be. So it is reasonable that a chief focus of catechesis is to help people prepare for, enter fully into, and reflect upon their experience of the Eucharist and the other sacraments.

Understanding that the liturgy is the "font and summit" of our lives heightens our awareness of the importance of preparing and celebrating it well. Reflecting on images, themes, and elements of our sacramental life and assisting people in connecting their experience of the liturgy with their daily lives, are essential to whole community catechesis. Such reflection invites people to profoundly embrace discipleship.

When people talk with me about what they find most meaningful in faith formation for adults, families, or children, the most common feeling they first express is excitement about their growing understanding of the Sunday Mass. Making connections between our prayer together at the Sunday assembly and daily life is terribly important; in fact, this dimension of faith formation is vital. "A little faith formation goes a long way," one of our staff likes to remind us. People echo that sentiment often. Understanding the ritual, symbolism, and rhythm of the feasts and seasons provides a rich context in which faith is nourished and can grow. As people are catechized, their lives begin to change in subtle but often profound ways.

Catechesis is about "helping (people) to know, to celebrate and to contemplate the mystery of Christ" (GDC #85). Faith formation that leads people to enter more fully into the liturgy and to live what they experience can take many forms:

- Small faith communities that prepare for the Eucharist by reflecting on the readings for the coming Sunday;

- Assemblies that explore elements of our prayer together or the feasts and seasons of the liturgical year (more on assemblies in chapter two);

- A parish bulletin that includes encouragement to reflect upon the experience of the liturgy, through a "Question of the Week" or some sort of guided reflection;

- Printed liturgical catechesis materials, available through the bulletin, newsletter, or a web site.

Ways to enhance the experience of the liturgy are almost as endless as the mystery that the liturgy celebrates. What is important is that we are mindful that catechesis helps bring people to the table of the Eucharist, be fully present at the table, and be sent forth as "living words" from the table.

"I have to thank you for your presentation last week," a woman said as we stood together in the serving line at a dinner for married couples. Our most recent gathering had been about the Eucharist. She went on to explain that the Mass had come alive for her as a result of the gathering and her reflection on our discussion that night. Over and over she found herself sharing what she had learned with her husband and her friends. "Now they want to hear your presentation for themselves," she said. "Will you be doing that presentation again any time soon?"

As people find that our celebration of the Eucharist doesn't need to be rote and that our prayer together is meant to be carried with us through each moment of our lives, not only are they changed but so are those around them.

## For Reflection/Discussion

• In what ways does your parish embrace a "lively baptismal and eucharistic spirituality"? (OHWB, p.5)

• Picture the average "person in the pew." What might that person say about the connection between the Sunday celebration of the Eucharist and everyday life?

## 2. PEOPLE SHARE THEIR FAITH

"The parish is...called to be a welcoming family where Christians become aware of being the people of God" (GDC #257). Some of us are fortunate to be part of such a parish; others have experienced such a parish while visiting family or friends. This kind of parish community makes people feel welcome and valued. Members recognize that their parish provides a context in which life is lived, all are loved, and in which they can discern their purpose in the world. Their experience of God and each other impels them to evangelize, to share the Good News with others. They have hope that goes beyond mere reason, and their hope is contagious.

I know that this description of a parish family sounds idealistic, and for many of us it is just that. Describing such a parish provides a vision of what true community can be, what a true community should be. When people's experience together is integral to their lives even when they are apart, they have formed community. Such a community becomes an entity greater than the sum of its parts. It is formed in God's image and likeness, and it cherishes and celebrates every person as essential to the whole. People in such a community live differently. While life continues to have its difficult moments, they have a sense of belonging and strength that assures them they are not alone.

This is the sort of "community" in which whole community catechesis takes place and that faith formation helps to form. As the community reflects on its relationship in Christ, every member is nurtured in faith, newcomers and long-timers alike. Each person is valued in a manner that says "not only do we care for you, but we care for you so deeply that we want you to grow in your love for Christ for the rest of your life."

What develops in response to this desire is different for each parish because it is a result of the community's self-reflection and discernment of its needs. The dimensions of whole community catechesis that we are exploring, and the various approaches that this book introduces, will be implemented differently by each community. The result, however, will be the same: a community that embraces faith formation as a lifelong endeavor. Such lifelong faith formation becomes part of the fabric of life in individuals, in families, and in the family of faith. Catechesis becomes a dynamic reality that changes and grows over time, just as the people within the parish change and grow over time.

## For Reflection/Discussion

- How are people encouraged to be actively involved in your parish community?
- Do people understand that being formed in faith is a lifelong endeavor? How is such an understanding being encouraged?

## 3. PARISHIONERS EMBRACE DISCIPLESHIP

Over the centuries, reflection upon the witness of Jesus' life and his mandate to wash one another's feet has resulted in a long tradition of service to those most in need, working toward justice and peace as expressed in the vision of Catholic social teaching. A preferential option for the poor and commitment to the service of other people grows out of conforming our lives to Christ. A catechesis that does not lead people toward living out their discipleship is not really catechesis at all.

Understanding Catholic social teaching helps people to connect the example of Christ—and of faithful people throughout the generations—to their own lives. The church, "above all, sees with profound sorrow 'an innumerable multitude of men and women, children, adults and old people and unique human beings, who suffer misery'" (GDC #17). Catechesis urges individuals to respond to this misery. Being formed in the ways of service and discipleship establishes a context for boldly living gospel truths in every situation and moment of our lives.

Faith formation cannot be contained in a classroom. Being formed in faith goes beyond "information" because it is rooted in Christian living that brings us out of ourselves, always pointing us toward others near and far. This is a catechesis of living discipleship. It makes sense to begin such catechesis when children are really young, so that as they grow in "age, wisdom, and grace," they naturally embrace this way of life.

> On the first day of vacation Bible school last summer, I walked into one of the activity centers just as a group of four- and five-year-olds were beginning the day. Their group leader began by saying that the activity they would be doing was about "mission." She asked if any of the children knew what that word meant. One child enthusiastically responded that "mission means to share our lives as Jesus did." The other children affirmed his response, and the leader replied that yes, mission is about sharing and caring for others just as Jesus did. Then the children were formed into groups that would package donated hygiene items into kits for women and children in downtown shelters.

Faith formation for us has become a living, breathing response to Christ's love through service, which helps us to understand and imitate him in reaching out to our sisters and brothers.

## For Reflection/Discussion

• What processes exist that can help your parishioners grow in their understanding of Catholic social teaching? Is there a group responsible for supporting justice formation?

• What opportunities for service and outreach currently exist for your parishioners?

## 4. Adults Are Active in Catechesis

We are never finished products! One of the most exciting dimensions of whole community catechesis is a movement toward adult faith formation. This is not to imply that catechesis for children and youth is not important; of course it is. Rather, the inclusion of adult catechesis in an ongoing manner simply completes a continuum that has been disrupted for many years: that of lifelong growing in and learning our faith.

Catechesis for adults, since it deals with persons who are capable of an adherence that is fully responsible, must be considered the chief form of catechesis. All the other forms, which are indeed always necessary, are in some way oriented to it (GDC #59).

I have to admit, when we first made a commitment to consistently offer adult faith formation, there were many within our community and around us who were convinced that few would participate. "It isn't worth your time," we were told repeatedly. "You'll see; people just won't come."

At the beginning it seemed the nay-sayers were right. Crowds were small and feedback was sparse. However, those who did attend and who were willing to react to what they experienced were encouraging. "Don't stop," they pleaded. "Give it time. It will build. This is important, so don't give up." The early participants were right. It did build, and we became better at discerning what people wanted and needed. Here are a few principles to keep in mind as you consider what your parish needs.

Adults learn in different ways, so they appreciate and need a variety of learning situations in which they can integrate concepts that are being presented with their lives at home, at work, in their leisure time, and in the parish itself. Whether gathering on parish grounds, joining a small faith community, or reflecting as individuals, adults will engage in ongoing faith formation only when they understand the benefits they can expect as a result of their participation. Once the community has experienced a variety of adult faith formation opportunities, those who enjoy the gatherings will invite friends and family to join them.

Some adults prefer to read at home and to decide individually what their new learning is calling them to act on. Others prefer small group discussions in which concepts are introduced and studied through interaction with others in a safe environment. Still others prefer large group, lecture-style presentations, possibly with some interaction with other persons, and/or with questions for reflection in the days that follow.

You might be amazed at the response of adults to very basic catechesis, and you will probably find that one thing easily leads to another and then another. In fact, once adult catechesis catches on, you'll find that the real task isn't deciding what to do but rather discerning what people need most and what can wait, since you'll have more ideas thrown at you than a single year could hold!

## For Reflection/Discussion

- What elements already exist within your parish that contribute to a community "vitally alive in faith"? (OHWB, p. 5)

- Are there adult faith formation opportunities available on a regular basis? What have been the results?

## 5. Catechesis Involves Everyone

"We are best when we are all together." When we take catechesis out of the classroom at least some of the time, and when we add adults to the mix, the catechetical climate begins to change. Bringing the whole community, or at least a representative sampling of the whole community, together for faith formation can be energizing and fun, while producing remarkable insights into and encouragement toward a lived faith.

The energy of an intergenerational catechetical gathering is much like a family coming home at the end of the day to enjoy dinner together, with each person sharing parts of his or her day's experience with the others at the table. Sure, it's messy sometimes, and sometimes things just don't turn out as we planned. Someone may be late or another might have had a really difficult day and needs special attention. One might be ill or another might have something special to share. Being together, sharing joys and challenges through the lens of faith, and growing together in discipleship builds both community and our life in Christ. It simply wouldn't be the same without the children or the teens or the adults. We're at our best when we're all together.

## For Reflection/Discussion

- At present, do people of all ages have the opportunity to grow in faith together in your parish?

- How does your community support faith sharing in small groups or in families?

## 6. The Catechumenate Is the Model

If we are concerned with supporting the development of faith-filled disciples, the process of faith formation will necessarily be multi-faceted. Such disciples possess observable characteristics that bear fruit throughout the course of their lives, for example:

- an ongoing relationship with God;

• a regular rhythm of full, conscious, and active participation in the Eucharist and the other sacraments;

• a daily life shaped by prayer and reflection on the paschal mystery of Christ's life, passion, death, and resurrection;

• a way of life rooted in the Word of God through reading and reflecting on Sacred Scripture;

• a basic understanding of and ability to explain essential beliefs as summarized in creedal statements;

• a moral behavior shaped by faith and expressed in the teaching of the church;

• an outpouring of service to others as an expression of living faith;

• a vital stewardship of the earth and of personal possessions;

• an active participation in the faith community with all of its benefits and responsibilities;

• a marked desire to share their love for God and the good news of the gospel.

This process of being formed and transformed by Christ throughout the span of our lives is what we commonly refer to as faith formation or catechesis.

An individual who embraces ongoing conversion will be in a constant state of development in one or many of the characteristics described above. In fact, these characteristics are facets of the character conferred in baptism. Initiation through the baptismal catechumenate pays close attention to ongoing growth in each of them. Likewise, the already baptized disciple must learn to recognize and invite personal growth in the above characteristics through a variety of processes and with the help of the Holy Spirit.

The initiating community understands itself as possessing, sharing, and continually growing in the characteristics of living discipleship. As we have already noted, such communities understand the primary place of the Eucharist as the central formation experience. They recognize the importance of providing catechesis that results in a profound eucharistic spirituality.

> About seven years ago, in my first year as the director of our catechumenate process, one of the sponsors shared her feelings as we approached the Triduum. She told me that in the week following the Rite of Election, as she recalled the moment when the catechumens signed the Book of the Elect, she came to envy those who were being "called by name." She wanted to be called by name. She wanted the refreshing waters of baptism. She wanted to know God's love as powerfully as the elect and candidates were coming to know God's love.
>
> She found herself in the grocery store, muttering to herself and fighting tears, singing over and over again the refrain we had sung as the catechumens had signed the book, as she pondered her own life in Christ and wondered what was missing. As she shared her story with the team and other sponsors, she was surprised to find others who were feeling the same emotions. In that gathering we spent time together helping each team member and sponsor recognize that they are already called by name and precious in God's sight.

In the years that have passed since that lenten season, I have watched people in our community come to recognize themselves as God's chosen ones, incorporated into Christ through the waters of baptism, and always precious in God's sight. With that recognition comes the desire to live our faith faithfully and fruitfully, and so the community celebrates, values, and flourishes in baptismal grace and living discipleship. It is less common now to hear people speak of how they wish they were special, and more common to hear how being a child of God calls them to an active response.

## For Reflection/Discussion

• Is the eucharistic liturgy a central learning moment in your parish? Why or why not?

• Does your parish see itself as possessing, sharing, and growing in the characteristics of living discipleship? In what ways? How could this be strengthened?

## 7. People Recognize and Celebrate Their Gifts

Imagine a parish where each person recognizes that everything we are and everything we have comes from God. With such understanding each person would be valued, and every member of the community would seek to share his or her gifts toward building up the body of Christ.

Maybe it isn't too difficult to imagine such a community. You may already see evidence of such understanding in your parish. Rooted in the knowledge of God's goodness and seeking to respond in gratitude, we come to realize that each of us need opportunities to prayerfully discern our gifts and to find ways to explore, develop, and offer these gifts within our families, our faith community, and the world.

When a parish encourages its members to share their gifts, catechesis and all the other ministries within the parish richly flow from the community itself. No longer are catechists simply the people who read the bulletin in late August and see an impassioned plea for someone to cover a third grade class in the fall. Catechists are people who possess the gift of teaching and who have been invited to share that gift within the community. Adult faith formation team members are not those who made the mistake of offering help when the DRE looked particularly harried. Rather, they are people who recognize in themselves a gift for envisioning and planning, and who wish to share that gift in the parish.

> A few years ago, a woman stopped in my office early one morning on her way to work. She wanted to express her disappointment with the confirmation preparation process. In a very detailed manner she offered her suggestions for improvement. As I listened to her, I recognized someone who cared deeply about our young people. I thanked her for her concern and asked if she would consider coming to the next Formation Advisory Commission meeting, to offer her suggestions and to find out more about how the group helps guide catechesis in our parish.
>
> Four years later as Gina was leaving the commission, having offered her insights about faith formation and having served as chairperson of the commission for two years, she teased that people had to be careful when they offered suggestions. They might find themselves, as she did, being asked to offer their gifts in ways they had never considered! The truth is that Gina discovered many of her gifts while she was part of the commission, and our community continues to benefit from her selfless giving.

## For Reflection/Discussion

- How does your parish help people discern their gifts?
- How are people invited to share their gifts? Is your parish a stewardship community?

## 8. The Parish Supports Households of Faith

Faith formation should be more like Mass than class. Look back at all that I have described up to this point, and a picture begins to develop of parish community catechesis that barely resembles the classroom model that has dominated the parish scene for the last generation and longer.

This picture includes faith formation processes that lead people toward eucharistic spirituality; children, youth, and adults learning and growing in faith together; gatherings that celebrate everyone in the community and benefit from the gifts of all; service and mission that are the result of intentional catechesis based on the church's social vision; processes that lead individuals and the community to embrace and embody Christian discipleship.

Whole community catechesis supports the development of households of faith, the family of faith supporting the family at home in a way that roots it in "profound human values" (GDC #255) and sustains it by building a web of care and love.

Now look at your own parish in relation to the eight dimensions as they have been outlined. Identify the areas that need the most attention and those in which there is much to celebrate. Make some serious notes before you leave this section.

### For Reflection/Discussion

- Whom might you invite to join this journey of transformation?

- What do you believe will be the largest obstacle to moving toward whole community catechesis? What elements within your parish's life hold the most promise?

CHAPTER TWO

# VEHICLES FOR THE JOURNEY

Now let us explore elements that can be used to implement this vision of faith formation. These elements are like vehicles that can take us along the path of whole community catechesis. Not all of them will be necessary for every parish, so each community will need to discern which vehicles are the best for its journey. Elements can be used in combination, helping people enrich their lives of faith through a "wide array of activities and resources designed to help adults more fully understand and live their faith" (OHWB, p. 5).

This section of the book will look at nine elements as separate units. Once an element has been described, a brief story will help illustrate what this element "looks like" in practice. Later, we'll consider how the elements can be used together or separately to address your parish needs. As each story unfolds, picture people in your parish participating, and imagine what could happen as a result.

## THE SUNDAY CELEBRATION

Helping people be transformed by their experience of the Sunday Eucharist is essential to the journey of discipleship through whole community catechesis. Realistically, if people attend Mass on Sunday but never reflect about what they hear, see, taste, touch, and do there, their faith will be dormant, stagnant.

In fact, many of the adults I speak with who become engaged in catechesis say that they never really "got" Mass before. Many faithfully attended every Sunday, but their attendance never became participation. Their minds and their hearts were never really engaged. Most will say that they didn't have a real relationship with Christ, one that affected the way they live.

Catechesis that helps people meet Christ is primary. Such a catechesis should aid them in developing a relationship with Christ that transforms their lives and helps them grow in their understanding of the Mass. There are many ways to assist individuals and families in making connections between their Sunday experience and their lives. We'll concentrate here on one way, and others will be described in later sections of this chapter.

Probably the simplest, yet potentially most profound piece of whole community catechesis, as presented by Bill

Huebsch in his book *Whole Community Catechesis in Plain English*, is the idea of a "Question of the Week." I will not address this in detail in this section, since the idea is well-developed in that book. However, I encourage you as you begin this exploration of the elements of whole community catechesis, to seriously consider establishing the Question of the Week or some guided reflection on the Sunday celebration within your community.

Not only does the Question of the Week invite individuals to reflect on the gospel and connect it to their own lives, it also establishes a pattern of faith reflection and sharing at parish meetings and assemblies that is crucial to the life of the community. When individuals and groups take the gospel to heart, amazing things begin to happen. It's that simple!

The story I told in chapter one (about the Faith Formation Advisory Commission's discussion), illustrates what can happen as a result of faith reflection and sharing as a regular part of parish meetings. The group that I described begins every meeting with at least a half hour of reflection, either on the gospel for the previous Sunday, a paragraph from a church document, or often both. Since we began this practice six years ago, the work of the commission has changed dramatically. The group has become, in effect, a small faith community, so much so that individual members speak of feeling a deep sense of loss in their lives when they discern that it is time to move to a different ministry.

Our reflection is based on a simple pattern:

• greeting and call to prayer;

• someone reads the gospel from the previous Sunday;

• someone else reads a paragraph from one of the documents to help the group focus;

• faith sharing and reflection on the readings follow, using these questions:

What words or phrases struck you most powerfully?

What do these passages/paragraphs say about who we are as church?

How might these passages/paragraphs influence our work tonight?

• The reflection and sharing end with a communal prayer.

One additional thought before we leave this important element. We cannot consider the centrality of the liturgy without speaking directly about the importance of celebrating the liturgy well. I realize many who read this book will be catechetical leaders, not music or liturgy directors. I hope, however, that all who are responsible for leadership within parishes will see whole community catechesis as an opportunity to strengthen the ties between liturgy, catechesis, and collaboration within parish leadership.

When people begin to consciously reflect on the Sunday celebration, they become more capable of full, conscious, and active participation. Look at this development in catechesis as an opportunity to strengthen your resolve to do everything possible to prepare and celebrate the liturgy with care. A community that is regularly reflecting on this celebration will respond profoundly.

## ASSEMBLIES

An assembly or gathering is an opportunity for people of all ages to come together to explore some element of the liturgy, our tradition, or a topic of particular interest. Sometimes, assemblies happen over a meal, helping people connect their table at home with the table of the Eucharist. Meal assemblies build upon the energy of table companionship, which Jesus clearly understood and used in teaching those around him.

In an assembly or gathering, those who are present are actively involved in taking the information presented and integrating it in their lives. People share their experiences at table, often with adults helping children to understand concepts, and children keeping adults "on track." The assembly models a special kind of dialogue. "As the children grow, exchange of faith becomes mutual and 'in a catechetical dialogue of this sort, each individual both receives and gives'" (GDC #227). Families learn, not only from one another, but from those with whom they share the experience.

See "Learning from Others" on page 62 for descriptions of dozens of assemblies that have been well received, ones you may want to adapt and use in your parish.

## PARALLEL PRESENTATION ASSEMBLIES

Some assemblies separate adults from children for at least part of the time. In such a gathering, the same topic or theme is explored in parallel presentations and activities, with an opportunity for families to share their experiences when they come back together. Let's look at a typical parallel assembly.

It's November, and our children have been learning about saints in their classrooms. The three days of Halloween, All Saints, and All Souls Day have just passed. Children's costumes haven't been boxed up yet, and the candy is still nearby. Some families have a new candle, lit only once at the parish's All Souls celebration for a family member who has died this year. Now, on November 4, families have gathered for "Hero Night," a night on which they will learn about saints as models and inspiration for our lives.

Everyone gathers in the cafeteria, and the evening begins with a song (For all the saints, who from their labors rest…). We pray the prayer known as the Breastplate of St. Patrick, and the leader for the evening invites people to share at table one thought about a saint that has inspired them.

After the sharing at tables, the children are taken aside for a little while for activities and age-appropriate catechesis, while the adults enjoy an interactive presentation about the origins of Halloween, All Saints, and All Souls, and about the ways in which we as Christian people first began to recognize the impact of saintly people in our lives: the martyrs, early teachers, family, friends, and the communion of saints.

Meanwhile, the children have been talking about saints in their lives, canonized saints and the "saints" around them, to whom they look for example. A small group of children dressed as people from another time move from room to room, telling the stories of a few familiar saints. Older children place huge sheets of newsprint on the hallway floors, trace someone's body, and paint the image as an icon of a saintly person.

Then, as the evening comes to a close, the children process back into the cafeteria to the music of "When the Saints Go Marching In." They are carrying their icon images and are led by the children dressed as saints of another era. The group of adults, teens, and children prays the Litany of the Saints, and each person is invited to greet the saints around them with a sign of peace.

## Intergenerational Assemblies

We have already explored several assemblies in which children and adults are separated for parallel experiences. Another type of assembly can be just as enriching and provides a wonderful context for continued dialogue and exploration following the assembly. Intergenerational assemblies, in which adults and children stay together for the presentation and activities, build on the excitement of sharing faith beyond generational boundaries. They build a common base of experience that can enhance the faith of individual participants and of families over time.

When we first began holding assembly catechetical sessions, we did so with a commitment to adults learning as adults, with the firm belief that when adults grow in their faith, such growth will positively affect the faith of the family. We still support this belief with dozens of adult faith formation opportunities throughout each year.

During a few assemblies each year, though, we invite adults and children to remain together, to discover things about the liturgy, the liturgical feasts and seasons, foundational stories of the people of God, or other elements of our faith. These assemblies are particularly enjoyable as the adults benefit from the unabashed interest of the children, and children experience catechesis side-by-side with their parents, grandparents, neighbors, and friends.

One of my favorite intergenerational evenings of all those we have experienced was "Vessels, Vestments, Symbols, and Signs," essentially a liturgical show and tell.

Our pastor began the evening by welcoming everyone and explaining that our prayer together can be enriched by better understanding the ritual moments and objects used during the liturgy. The littlest ones among us, those in pre-school and grade one, were taken to a specially prepared room, and our parochial vicar and a gifted group of early childhood catechists led them through the same kind of tour that the older children and adults would enjoy in the church and surrounding rooms.

We divided the remaining group into three sub-groups (with about 125 in each group). Each group moved to three stations through the course of the night. They explored the main body of the church with a group leader, who explained the holy oils, the altar, ambo, presider's chair, sacred vessels, and the role of music ministry. A second station was held in the priest's sacristy where the pastor explained the use of the sacramentary, lectionary, ordo, and vestments. The third station began at the reconciliation chapel, then moved to the baptismal font where one of our deacons reminded participants of their baptismal promises and gave a quick overview of the liturgical year.

Recently, as our church was renovated and rededicated, people have begun asking for a "Vestments, Vessels, Symbols, and Signs, Part Two," in which we can explore the elements again, this time in a beautiful new space that teaches us as we celebrate.

## ADULT FAITH FORMATION

Where adult catechesis is concerned, one size definitely does not fit all! In exploring this dimension of whole community catechesis in chapter one, we recognized that adults need and respond to a variety of styles of being formed and informed. As you begin to consider this element of whole community catechesis, take some time to read or review the United States bishops' document on adult faith formation, *Our Hearts Were Burning within Us*.

Look at the six elements of catechesis presented there:

• knowledge of the faith,

• liturgical life,

• communal life,

- missionary spirit,
- prayer, and
- moral formation.

Think about the ways your parish already supports faith formation in these six categories. Breaking catechetical processes and needs into such categories helps us recognize the many ways in which we are already supporting parish adults in their ongoing relationship with Christ and the church. It also gives us a quick, visual way of finding areas that need our attention.

Planning and preparing adult faith formation can be quite enjoyable when we are willing to relax, listen, and invite people to share opportunities with us. Remember those principles we mentioned in chapter one? Adults will only come to a gathering when they understand its relevance to their lives and when they are comfortable with the style of presentation. Not every adult will come to every catechetical gathering. One size does not fit all!

Let's look at some common modes of providing adult faith formation, and then at one example of a process as it has developed over time:

- printed catechetical pieces in the bulletin, newsletter, or on the parish website. An example of this is a weekly question and answer column;

- the "Question of the Week" or a guided reflection on the Sunday readings that invites a faith response;

- small faith communities;

- retreat/renewal processes (a little more on this later in this chapter);

• a series or class on topics such as Church History, Liturgy and Rites, Apologetics, Just Faith, or Communities of Salt and Light;

• adult assemblies paired with children's activities on the same topic;

• book clubs and discussion groups, such as "Reading Between the Wines;"

• married couple dinners, marriage and baptism preparation processes, ministry formation and training.

It is also very important to offer opportunities for integrating what is being "preached" through catechesis and what is being lived: service and outreach opportunities, community-building functions, processes that invite a response to identified needs within the parish or local civic community, justice formation and works of justice at the local, national, and global levels.

A few years ago, women in our parish began talking with our pastor and staff about a women's Bible study that took place in a neighboring church. It was a comfortable morning that included music, fellowship, a presentation, table sharing, and prayer. The environment in the room was very special, with many women's touches: candles, table arrangements, color, and a theme that was carried through a season or series of presentations. Child care was graciously provided, and the participants were made to feel totally at home.

"Why," they asked, "couldn't we have something like this at our parish?" They went on to explain that they had initially enjoyed the experience at the neighboring church, then were confused at some of the things that were presented as well as angry that their own parish wasn't providing something like this.

I asked if any of them would be willing to help bring this

about. "Yes! Of course!" was the unanimous reply. So a team was started, and an invitation for others to join appeared in the bulletin. The original planning team grew to twenty-two, and the team divided into task groups, one group for hospitality, another for publicity, one for formation and programming, and another for registration and table management. By the time the first season of "Grace-full Women" made its debut, it seemed every woman I met was talking about the new process.

The team had decided to offer a six-part series in the fall on Thursday mornings, with child care provided. The initial reservations were for forty participants. How stunned we all were when, on the first morning, sixty women of all ages arrived! A few brought infants in strollers to the delight of the grandmothers in the group. A larger room was arranged for the second Thursday, and it was a good thing because eighty women came. The group stayed at an enjoyable number of eighty to ninety persons for the rest of the series. The participants weren't always the same, as people's lives do include schedule conflicts and choices that must be made, but the number remained consistent throughout the fall.

A Sunday afternoon winter tea, a way of inviting working women into the process, had one hundred and fifty reservations. Despite the worst ice storm of a decade, seventy-five women still participated!

When the second season of Grace-full Women was taking place, a group of participants began to talk about things they wish they understood about our faith, the "hows and whys" of our tradition. So, in between seasons two and three, we held "Quench Your Thirst Days," in which we wove the stories of the early days of the church, explaining how Scripture came to be, how the Mass developed, how the liturgical seasons took shape, and so on.

Grace-full Women has taught me much about adult faith formation. I have been reminded again and again of the importance of listening to the adults of our community, and

I have learned to trust their insights and desires. I have found that when we celebrate and invite people to share the gifts they possess, the work is made light and joyful. I have experienced the deep desire of women of all ages and states of life to grow in love of God and one another, and I have been renewed by the power of their shared experiences and support for each other along the journey. We have been richly blessed because a group of women cared enough to share their ideas and themselves with our community. Now, the men of the parish are beginning to ask, "Could we do something similar, less frilly of course, but something to feed our spirits?"

## CHILDREN AND YOUTH

As the catechetical climate begins to be transformed in the parish community, elements that were previously in place often experience new life and energy. Children's programs will find adult catechists who not only have discovered a gift for teaching, but who possess a renewed love of their faith. Youth find adults who are actively involved in their own relationship with Christ and who are willing to share their journey with teens. Parents no longer feel at a loss when their children ask them questions; they aren't worried that they won't know the answers. If they aren't sure of a response, they are well-acquainted with resource people who will help them find the answers they seek.

Depending on the parish and the direction you and your advisory team take, the children's program may be transformed into something vastly different from a classroom program. Classroom instruction may continue, however, but the program will benefit from catechists whose lives are being transformed through active participation in ongoing catechesis.

Faith formation for children and youth benefits in other ways as well. Think about the potential impact of a series of gatherings like the "Hero Night" that was described earlier. Children are taught concepts built on processes of discovery and fun. Youth realize that they are being asked to do things that the rest of the community is also doing. Small faith communities, retreat experiences, service, and outreach: there are many opportunities for teens and adults to learn about Christ together, or for young people to learn skills that will serve them well into their adult years. And as the opening of chapter one indicated, teens can be actively involved in helping to shape catechesis for the whole community.

Our annual lenten series has developed into an exciting process of spiritual formation for children, youth, and adults. Each of the Friday evenings of Lent begins with a fish fry, drawing people from throughout the area. The fish fry is followed by the Stations of the Cross. Families are rediscovering this form of prayer; the stations are sometimes led by youth and other times by adults. The stations are followed by faith formation for children, teens, and adults. Children are gathered into age groups, from age three through twelve. Our youth sometimes have a parallel presentation; other times they join the adults for their presentation. Often they also help with the children's activities for the evening.

This past Friday was one of those nights that "glowed." Our series this year was based on the psalm for the coming Sunday, so Friday's presentation, "Taste and See the Goodness of the Lord," provided a way for participants to consider the importance of beauty in raising our vision to God. The adults were treated to three mini-presentations.

One was similar to a retreat, as the speaker asked us to consider all the beauty around us that reminds us of God's presence. Her presentation included slides of nature, people, and our newly renovated church building. The other two speakers were artists who were involved in the church renovation. They explained how the community's worship space committee had prayerfully discerned elements for the new space, and how prayer had inspired their own work.

Meanwhile, our youth and children traveled to four "stations" in the school building. At one station, two parishioners led the participants in celebrating the beauty of sung prayer. At another, the participants enjoyed a demonstration of stained glass in the making, and at another, they painted ornaments that will hang on Christmas trees on the church grounds next year. At the fourth station a brief video about St. Joseph (it was St. Joseph's feast day) reminded the children that Jesus probably learned Joseph's carpentry skills by working side by side with this saint who is a model for our response to God's call.

At the end of the evening, as the adults concluded their time together, they were given a description of the children's activities for the evening so the parents could talk with their children about their experiences on the way home. Is it any wonder the lenten series has become such a favorite?

## SERVICE TO OTHERS

It isn't possible to truly follow Christ without serving our brothers and sisters. What we sometimes forget is that such service, especially when we are offered an opportunity to reflect upon the experience, is formative. We learn by doing.

People who are in a relationship with Christ will want to express that relationship through outreach to the poor of our community family through works of justice and peace, through connection to the church in other places within their town or city and globally, and through service within the parish community. Providing opportunities for such mission, outreach, and service is a vital element of catechesis. Very often generations can serve side-by-side. The impact of people of faith from all age groups, ministering together to other sisters and brothers in our community, generates bonds of love transcending any differences that may exist.

> About five years ago, our parish established a twin relationship with a community in Mangua, Nicaragua. At first, it seemed like a simple idea, despite the distance not only geographically but also in culture and lifestyle. Over time, this distance has gradually lessened. We are united through relationships built between people, as groups from each community have visited the other. We have grown closer, too, through projects that raise money or donations of material resources such as school supplies, books, health products, and building supplies.
>
> One of the wonderful bi-products of the twin relationship has been the variety of opportunities for our children, teens, and adults to work together for a common purpose. Projects like an annual garage sale and children's mission activities (connected with the witness of youth and adults who have visited our community in Nicaragua) have helped to develop ties within our parish and with parishioners who are far from us globally but now close to our hearts.

## A SUMMER CATECHETICAL OPTION

When we speak of changing the catechetical climate in a parish and begin to look at faith formation as an ongoing response to a personal relationship with Christ, alternative options for children's instruction can easily follow. One such option is a summer catechetical program.

We began the summer option in its present form in 1997.

At that time, our parish also had a Wednesday evening and a Sunday morning program that took place during the school year. The parish had experienced a pilot summer catechetical process a few years before. Some families that had participated were anxious for a program from which many more could benefit and with more follow-up opportunities for families throughout the year. The diocesan graded course of study (the curricular requirements for each grade level) needed to be covered. We also wanted children to experience many forms of prayer through the course of the two-week session. When we committed to a summer session in 1997, none of us was prepared for the exciting consequences.

The summer option has grown to such an extent that our Wednesday option is no longer necessary. Two-thirds of our children in public schools participate in the summer faith formation program, with their families making a commitment to ongoing faith formation throughout the year through assemblies and/or adult catechesis.

The summer process offers longer formation periods with less time between. Rather than saying, "Remember what we discussed three weeks ago," a catechist can say, "Remember what we talked about yesterday." The children who participate in the sessions enjoy their time with friends, in an atmosphere that lets them explore themes and concepts in a manner rarely possible during the winter months. Not only do they have more time together, but each day includes music, art, drama, recreation, community-building, and time with our priests, deacons, and youth minister.

Catechists are either certified teachers or certified catechists, so faith formation is carried out with skill. Parents are deeply involved as aides, activity leaders, and administrative support. Some parents take a week's vacation to be involved in the summer session. Families carpool and parents and younger siblings enjoy being part of the opening and closing prayers, with each group taking a turn at preparing them.

This summer option has had many amazing results. Children learn and retain more, and their families live their faith more consistently. Parents and children appreciate the realistic approach of summer catechesis, since weekday evenings and weekends during the school year are filled with many distracting activities. Summer is fun! The children look forward to their time together. They and their families enjoy gathering during the year for assemblies that reinforce their faith.

Our summer session always ends with a gathering of all the children, their parents, and younger siblings, for the regular noon Mass on Friday afternoon. Last summer, on the Monday following the close of one of our summer sessions, an older gentleman came quietly into our office, asking if he could speak with someone about what he experienced the week before.

He sat down at a chair near my desk and explained that he was from a neighboring parish and had happened to come to noon Mass the Friday before. He was amazed at the life that surrounded him as the children and their families came in for Mass. Especially wonderful, he said, was the joy the children seemed anxious to share. "What have they been doing?" he wondered. Is this CCD? It certainly didn't seem like any CCD program he had ever known.

The regular daily Mass attendees seemed happy to be joined by so many joyful children and parents. Would I be willing to speak with his pastor about what was taking place here? "He should know about this!" I assured him I would be willing to share the program with his pastor. I also mentioned that other neighboring parishes had sent catechists, children, and families to our program as a way of beginning summer programs for their parishioners.

## HOME-BASED CATECHESIS

We catechetical leaders often remind parents of the promise they made at their child's baptism, that they would be the first and best teachers of the faith. Yet in most parishes today, little is done to support parents who want to take an active role in the catechesis of their child.

When the whole community is involved in assemblies, adult faith formation, intergenerational gatherings, sacramental preparation, and the like, home-based catechesis suddenly becomes a viable option for children's instruction. Most parents are very capable of using a religion text, especially when there are also parent support meetings, community assemblies, and service opportunities. All of these create a rich texture of elements that truly form the children in the faith.

A few years ago three small, rural parishes began making preparations to merge into one parish. The pastors began to talk with the parishioners about the many facets of their lives that would begin to intertwine, and how the communities could be joined in ways that would benefit from the resources they would soon be sharing with others. The pastors hired a Director of Religious Education to help them make the shift to combined faith formation opportunities for all the members of the three parishes, soon to be one.

Sr. Rita, the DRE they found, took time to become acquainted with parishioners in all three parishes, and for the first year, nothing in any of the parish programs changed. Sr. Rita enhanced the existing programs with a few adult faith formation opportunities, and she began to talk with other DREs and the staff in the diocesan Office of Religious Education about options her parishioners could consider as they planned for a combined future. The diocesan director suggested that she visit with me to learn about our summer option, and with another DRE who has a well-developed, home-based option.

Sr. Rita did her homework, and then asked the other DRE and me to assist her in presenting the options to the parishioners in the three parishes. Sr. Angela, the DRE with the home-based option, and I greatly enjoyed two evening meetings in which parishioners were given information about three options that would be offered to them for the coming year. One option would be a Sunday evening classroom option during the school year; the second was the summer option with ongoing faith formation for families and adults; the third, a home-based option, included monthly support meetings for parents, like the process at Sr. Angela's parish.

When registrations were completed, a small number of families had chosen the school year classroom option. Many more had chosen either summer or home-based catechesis, citing the flexibility and realistic nature of both processes. One of the parents stopped me as I left an evening meeting and said, "I am really impressed that you, Sr. Rita, and Sr. Angela all seem to respect us as parents. None of you said anything that didn't speak of trust and a desire to support us. That's a wonderful gift! Thank you!"

Any time I meet with parents and we speak of options for faith formation and of the many catechetical processes available to them, I remind them that anything they do to grow in their relationship with Christ and to nurture their faith will have a wonderful effect on their families. What we want to do by offering catechetical options is to support every member of our parish community on their journey of faith and to support parents in their role as proclaimers of the faith with their children. Not only do parents appreciate the support that is offered, but eventually most become actively involved in helping to offer catechetical opportunities to the whole community.

## Sacramental Preparation Assemblies

You have already been introduced to assembly ideas that help people make connections between their everyday lives and the liturgy. From walk-throughs of sacramental celebrations, to explorations of the church, to reflections on the Sunday readings, catechesis that intentionally builds connections between liturgical prayer and the rest of life is an important element of whole community catechesis.

When you apply the structure of an assembly to sacramental preparation, the whole community is enriched and the whole family is involved with the sacrament. Intergenerational assemblies and those with parallel presentations—adults in one place and children in another— can be very effective for preparing children for their first reception of the sacraments of reconciliation and eucharist or for their confirmation. These assemblies are also very effective for couples preparing for marriage and for parents as they prepare for the baptism of their children.

While such gatherings have a primary intended "audience," it is always beneficial to invite the whole community to participate. Not only do all who participate grow in their understanding of the sacrament, but an additional dimension of community develops. People who are not connected to those preparing for sacraments through family ties become connected through the family of faith.

One year, at a "walk-through" of the sacraments of healing, I explained to about five hundred children and adults that the sacrament of reconciliation had developed over many centuries. It was the result of reflecting and praying over Jesus' many examples of forgiveness. I explained that in the early centuries of the church, one of the major obstacles was apostasy (publicly denying one's faith). When someone denied the faith in a time of persecution and then later asked to return, what was the community to do?

A girl, probably in the fourth or fifth grade, asked, "If all the people in the early church denied the faith, how could the pope and bishops today be linked to Peter?" Wow! What a question! I quickly reassured her that not all the faithful had denied the faith, and also thanked her for thinking so hard about what we were discussing. It was amazing to hear the questions that followed, not only from the children but from the adults as well. It was as though the child's question had opened the eyes and ears of all those present. We all learned a great deal about reconciliation from one another that evening.

When people make connections between the liturgy and their lives, they begin to integrate prayer into their lives. Their growing comfort with the prayers and rites of the sacraments helps them establish regular rhythms of prayer and fuller participation in the actual celebration of the sacraments.

## RETREAT AND RENEWAL PROCESSES

When considering elements that encourage people to grow in their relationship with Christ, don't forget the retreat and renewal processes. Whether it's a weekend retreat, a day of renewal, an evening of prayer, membership in a small faith community or in a Scripture study group, such opportunities give parishioners the chance to step aside from their normal routine. The combination of prayer, peer witness, and faith sharing can change lives.

A parishioner recently shared a story with me that shows the power of a parish-based retreat. He was speaking about coming to terms with his father's cancer eight years earlier. When his father was diagnosed with the illness, the whole family was affected. Knowing this, the man's father had encouraged him to take stock of his own life and to focus on what was really important.

Throughout his father's illness and eventual death, this man knew he had to make important changes in his life. For eight years he struggled with this, but it was on a men's weekend retreat that he "really let Christ into his life," and his life was changed.

## Essential Elements

Go back to the beginning of this chapter and briefly review each of the elements, the vehicles that take us on the path of whole community catechesis. Which vehicles will be absolutely necessary for your parish? Which will enhance the journey over time? Your parish community will need to discern which of the vehicles will best support each person along the path toward living discipleship.

In my experience, these are the essential elements.

• Connection to the Sunday liturgy. We need to make that connection, either through the Question of the Week or in some other, regular manner.

• Assemblies. Whole community catechesis is not possible without some opportunities for people to deepen their connection with one another as they are invited into a transforming relationship with Christ. We are communal people; our connections to one another lead us to experience Christ in our midst. While there will be individuals who will not participate in an assembly, those individuals may be deeply transformed through their interaction with others who do participate. The community is strengthened through the assembly experience, through which adults, youth, and children are invited to continual conversion in Christ.

• Adult catechesis. Discipleship is demanding, and adults who are conforming their lives to Christ will understand that the need to continue growing in faith never ends. Adult faith formation is essential.

• Children and youth. Because we are devoting time and energy to adult catechesis doesn't mean we give less attention to younger members of the community. What is important is to choose the catechetical options that are a good fit for your parish, those that support lifelong growth in faith.

• Service. We act in response to our love of God and we grow in love of God through serving our sisters and brothers in God's family.

Discern the other elements that will enhance your community's journey. A summer catechetical option, home-based catechesis, assembly-based sacramental preparation, and retreat and renewal processes are elements that may enhance a community's journey along the path of discipleship. Each community will need to discern which of those elements will best support the "whole" of whole community catechesis. Side-by-side with that discernment will be decisions about how to begin and sustain the essential elements described above. Chapter three will suggest structures and processes for this discernment.

## For Reflection/Discussion

• Which elements mentioned in this chapter are most needed in your parish if whole community catechesis is to take root?

• Which elements are already "in place" in your parish? What has been the response of your parishioners so far?

CHAPTER THREE

# PLANNING AND IMPLEMENTING

You know the path you want to take. You have explored the vehicles that might be used for the journey. Now you need to discern which vehicles will be the most beneficial for your parish. You'll need to think about where you are, where you hope to go, and how you will get there. As with any good trip, you need to include others in the planning, so that the journey itself will meet everyone's needs, hopes, and dreams.

If whole community catechesis is to be a path toward living discipleship for the whole parish, planning and implementation will need the active participation of members of the community. If you don't already have one, now is a good time to form an advisory group, commission, or committee. If you do have one, now is the perfect opportunity to reenergize the group, possibly add new members, and provide formation for them as a vital link in this process.

Let's look at ways to discern, invite, and form a faith formation advisory group. We'll then see how that group can provide essential input as you begin or continue on the journey toward whole community catechesis.

## FORMING A TEAM

Finding and inviting individuals to be involved in the planning and implementation of whole community catechesis can be an exciting process. The group you invite doesn't need to be large, and no previous experience is necessary. You may already have an advisory group. If so, consider what follows in relation to the group you have in place; this would be a perfect time to add members or to provide some additional formation for the team. If you're beginning an advisory group from scratch, here are some things to consider.

• Decide on your "ideal" number of members. Typically eight to ten members will give you enough variety in perspectives and experience while keeping discussions productive. You could easily begin with fewer members and add additional people once the community understands more about the impact of catechesis.

• Seek to build a group that represents the community through diversity in age and involvement in existing organizations and ministries. Familiarity with catechesis and/or interest in helping to build something of value for the parish is a real plus.

• Consider inviting a few people you know well and a few you don't know. It may be tempting to begin with familiar faces only, but that will limit the perspectives from which input arises. It is good to have a few with whom you have a positive relationship, and let them set the tone for open, honest dialogue, critique, and envisioning. Also ask the pastoral leadership team for names of potential members. They may be aware of other people with special gifts and talents who understand the many facets of parish life.

Often people are willing to try being part of a team like this if they are given the opportunity. Invite potential members to consider a short term or a discernment period of six months to a year. Once people have participated in foundational formation and they begin to see plans coming together, they are likely to commit to a term of two to three years.

Invite potential members to an information meeting where you can explain what you hope will develop over time, and what the role of the advisory team will be. You can lead them in a typical faith reflection/envisioning experience like the one detailed in chapter two (The Sunday Celebration) and through that experience, elicit initial ideas. If you have an advisory group already in place, consider holding a meeting in which the group discusses its role and in which it is invited to offer suggestions for the future. Members will appreciate an opportunity to share their perceptions of what's happening in the parish.

Once the group has been identified, invited, and has committed to a period of service, it's time to map out a formation process for the advisory team.

Our Faith Formation Advisory Commission has been developing and growing over a period of about eight years. We now have two teen members (a freshman and a junior in high school), two young adults (one single, one married with young children), three parents of children in our parish school, two parents of children in public elementary schools, two adults who have teenage children, and a senior citizen.

Last year as we were discussing ways of building connections between middle-school catechesis, youth ministry, and "real life," Molly (you met her in my opening story) spoke from her heart. She said, "If you think that the junior high students really feel comfortable talking about their faith, you've got another think coming."

When someone asked why she said this, she went on to explain, "It's like you enter seventh grade and suddenly everyone's afraid to really talk about things with you. Teachers and parents—everyone seems to think that kids will ask questions they can't answer, or that the kids won't want to hear honest answers, so everyone seems to avoid the real stuff. I know people whose friends go to other churches, and they don't know how to explain what we believe, or why, and they get confused. When they ask their parents, the parents just look at them and say, "Don't ask me, I don't know!""

Just a few months later, Molly was serving as a sixth-grade aide in our summer program. One day, as I made the rounds talking with each of the middle school classes, I could feel the warmth coming from Molly's corner of the room. She beamed with happiness, knowing that her input had been taken to heart. The children in the class asked all sorts of things, just as we were told they would, and they were outwardly appreciative that someone wasn't afraid of their questions! I was grateful that our teen commission members understand their perceptions are vital and that we truly want to learn from them.

## For Reflection/Discussion

- Do you have a faith formation advisory group? What is its role and how does it function?

- Is it time to form or re-form your team? Does your group represent the diversity of your community?

### Formation for the Team

Once you have a faith formation advisory team in place, it is time to provide the group with their own formation that will help them develop a vision of living discipleship through whole community catechesis.

The reflection/faith sharing process described in chapter two, using the Sunday Gospel, Question of the Week, and a paragraph from one of the church's documents will encourage team members to develop a vision of what effective catechesis could look like in your parish. Over the last five years, our Faith Formation Advisory Commission members have read portions of the *General Directory for Catechesis*, *Our Hearts Were Burning within Us*, the *Rite of Christian Initiation of Adults*, the *Constitution on the Sacred Liturgy*, *Renewing the Vision*, *Stewardship: the Disciple's Response,* and the *Constitution on the Church in the Modern World*. The reflective reading the group has done has a cumulative effect on members of the group and on our parish. Our discussions have become rich and deep, and the group's reflection has an immediate and lasting impact on our community, since our faith formation processes come directly from the advisory commission's dialogue.

Consider establishing an annual day of reflection for the team. This is a wonderful opportunity to begin the year, and it is beneficial to have extended time to reflect and share. Such a day builds trust and a collaborative spirit among members, and the tasks of the group can begin in a prayerful atmosphere. This is a good time to integrate formation to strengthen spirituality for ministry, and a wonderful way to establish a sense of common purpose within the team.

Another option is to schedule a series of meetings, with each focusing on one dimension or element of whole community catechesis. You can use this book as your guide for these meetings.

During our first few years we tried to address all of the facets of formation at one meeting, and we found ourselves tired and frustrated. It was simply too much for members to take in all at once. We eventually mapped out these meetings a year in advance and stayed with our plan as closely as possible, with the flexibility to address issues as they arose.

## For Reflection/Discussion

- If you have an advisory team in place, does the group regularly study portions of key catechetical documents?

- How do you currently decide what kind of catechesis the parish needs? Does your decision include input from members of your community? How might forming an advisory group, or strengthening a current group, enhance catechesis in your parish?

## Advisory Team Meetings

An advisory group is crucial to successful planning. The more you hear members' thoughts and the greater their enthusiasm for what develops, the more the whole community is likely to be engaged in catechesis. Let me describe a typical meeting and a typical year, so that you can see how this works.

A typical meeting has a predictable pattern that provides for reflection, sharing, reporting, evaluating, and idea-gathering. While I say this, I should also caution that some of our best work has taken place during a meeting that was anything but "typical." Remember that the real work of the group is to provide input and ideas for catechesis that will engage the whole community. Often such ideas will be a direct result of the reflection that happens at the beginning of the meeting. The rest of the group's tasks can be accomplished either in brief or at another time.

The meeting begins with the reflection structure described in chapter two. This usually takes about fifteen minutes. Next, a brief report brings team members up to date. (A detailed report is provided in advance, via email.) Thirdly, we focus on a particular facet of faith formation in our parish (for example, children's catechesis, youth ministry, or adult faith formation). Parish staff members who share responsibility for this facet are also invited.

Usually the opening reflection is related to the aspect of faith formation we are discussing, and it gives direction to our conversation and offers us a vision that guides our dialogue. We discuss where we are in relationship to that vision, and how we can adjust what we are doing to best support whole community catechesis.

Finally, any additional thoughts or concerns are shared, and the meeting ends with a brief prayer or blessing. Meetings always include a snack, provided by one of the members, so the gathering usually doesn't come to an abrupt halt. We stay and enjoy each other's company over food. The whole meeting lasts approximately ninety minutes.

While catechesis happens year-round, our advisory group's year begins in August and runs through June. The elements of catechesis that have already been planned for the summer and fall are the result of conversations from the previous year, so there is a continuous cycle of input, dialogue, reflection, planning, and implementation. (See the Appendix for a schedule of a typical year of meetings.)

## For Reflection/Discussion

• How might the parish leaders in your parish be better formed for the ministry they provide? Is their input valued and utilized?

• Are your meetings prayerful and collaborative? What steps can you take to make them more so?

## WHAT COMES NEXT?

Once you have a formation team in place, it's time to ask: where are we now? Where do we hope to go? How will we get there? It's time to map out the first leg of your journey.

You now have a group of travel consultants who will help you discern which vehicles are most appropriate. You need to take a careful look at where you are now before you begin to map a course for the future. Once you have an understanding of your current position, you'll be ready to create an itinerary that includes the vehicles you will use for the first portion of your trip.

To determine where you are now can be a simple process or one that needs some time and prayer. Do you already have certain processes in place (intergenerational gatherings, Questions of the Week, and so on)? If yes, you might want to survey parishioners to determine their effectiveness.

The object of such a survey is to hear the thoughts and dreams of your community, even if this means hearing things you don't want to hear. Keep an open mind and heart, and remember that much can be discovered from feedback that initially seems negative.

If you have not previously offered faith formation beyond a children's catechetical program, now is a wonderful time to invite parishioners to express their hopes and dreams. Don't be surprised if they seem unable to articulate what they want. When we first began asking parishioners what sorts of faith formation opportunities they desired, most could not be specific. They simply wanted something. After the first two years of adult and intergenerational gatherings, people began asking for more specific types of processes. It simply took time and experience for parishioners to understand what they needed or to have an idea of what is possible.

With your advisory team, prayerfully reflect on the vision of your parish on a journey of discipleship. Are you on the path that leads to whole community catechesis? (Use the reflection questions at the end of each section of chapter one to determine your current situation with regard to each of the dimensions of whole community catechesis.)

Gather the information you receive from surveys, conversations with parishioners, and the vision of your formation team, and spend an evening or Sunday afternoon with as many interested people as you can gather to discern where you are right now. Is your whole community engaged in a living relationship with Christ; are you a community "vitally alive in faith"? (OHWB, p. 5).

Ideally, your pastor, other pastoral staff, and your pastoral council will participate in this gathering. It is important for all who are involved in parish leadership to share the vision that you and your team will be working toward. Once you have determined where you are currently, it is time to consider which elements to put into place. Which vehicles will be most appropriate for your community's journey of discipleship?

## Which Vehicles Will You Use?

How will we enter the path of whole community catechesis? In chapter two we looked at the essential elements of whole community catechesis and at some that are optional. Each parish has to determine which elements will best suit its needs. Begin reasonably, taking on only as much as you believe you can do well in a calendar year. Choose elements that will most easily invite people to connect their experience of Sunday Eucharist with the rest of their lives, with the goal of inviting people to a deeper relationship with Christ. Begin with a few assemblies the first year, possibly one a month or one every two months. Once people have experienced this kind of catechesis, they will better grasp the joy of lifelong faith formation.

Once you have decided which elements to employ, it's time to plan for the next six months to a year. Map out in calendar form what will take place, then work backwards to develop a planning calendar, listing the tasks that need to be accomplished and the people who can take responsibility for them. Be as detailed as you can, while maintaining flexibility to adjust and adapt as you experience processes for the first few months. Take photos of assemblies and keep a journal of the feedback, ideas that surface, and people who offer their help for future events.

Your journey has begun! Enter into it as fully as you can, and remember that, as with many such experiences, there will probably be unexpected discoveries along the way. Like the disciples on the road to Emmaus, you and your community may find your hearts burning within you as you begin the walk with Christ on the path of discipleship.

## Looking Back, Looking Ahead

Once you have entered the path of whole community catechesis, once you and your advisory group have discerned which elements will best suit your parish, and once you have experienced the first few months on the journey, it's time to begin planning the next leg of your journey together.

It's easy to get caught up in the implementation of whole community catechesis and forget to evaluate what is taking place. It will be vitally important, though, to listen, to watch, to ask, and to involve more people in dreaming for the future. We have learned much since we began offering assemblies and adult faith formation, but only because we have been willing to think critically and because we have responded when people offered suggestions. We haven't done everything people asked us to do, but we have certainly listened for running themes, common questions, and consistent critique.

By being willing to listen and asking our advisory commission to be eyes and ears for the parishioners, the processes that we have designed are meeting identified needs in a way that we believe will draw people into a fuller understanding of themselves as disciples of the Lord.

Once you have established a pattern of listening, have made connections to the Sunday liturgy, and have experienced faith formation assemblies, assess where you are and consider what might benefit your parish in the future. This is the way whole community catechesis is sustained over time.

Look at where you are (a different place than the last time you did this) and where you wish to go. Consider the elements you've employed and look at adaptations or adjustments that might strengthen your efforts. Look at additional elements that may be appropriate in the coming year and map out the next leg of your journey. Continue to involve people in your planning, especially new parishioners or those who voice enthusiasm for what they are experiencing.

Pray often to the Holy Spirit and look out! You will likely be amazed at what transpires. Be prepared for your own life to change and for a great transformation within your parish community. Be open to new ways for involving every person in your parish in the journey to whole community catechesis. Even after seven years, Immaculate Heart of Mary Parish is still finding new ways to involve adults in lifelong faith formation.

"Reading between the Wines (or Coffee or Tea)" is the latest adult process to find its way to our calendar. For years, parishioners have told us about books they have read, and how their reading has led them to questions about our faith, or to a deeper spirituality that they would like to share with others. "Why not begin a book club?" has been a common question, and so now that our parish facilities include a few nicely furnished parlor rooms, we are responding to the request.

The books we discuss will be of two sorts. We'll be reading books that are popular but controversial due to the questions they raise for people of faith. Our pastor enjoys helping people delve deeply into the reasons we believe as we do, and he loves equipping people to respond to the questions of others around them, so he will facilitate many of these discussions. The other type of discussion will center on books of a spiritual nature that lend themselves to group study and sharing. If those who have asked for such a process are a good indication, "Reading between the Wines" will appeal to adults of many ages and of varied life experience. We hope and pray that we engage people in a way that is life-giving and relevant to their lives.

# CHAPTER FOUR

# LEARNING FROM OTHERS

This chapter includes ideas that have been effective for other parishes, as well as worksheets for planning, discernment resources, and suggestions for evaluating whole community catechesis within your parish. Feel free to adapt any of these to fit your own parish situation.

## PARALLEL ASSEMBLIES

Typically the assembly begins with prayer. Sometimes this is formal evening prayer and at other times a simple prayer to gather us in Christ's presence. The children are called forward in age groups, and their catechists take them to their activity areas. Adults enjoy a speaker, often with opportunities for faith sharing or discussion. Those adults who are parents end the evening by picking their children up at the activity area, where they are given a handout that describes what the children have done during the presentation time. This sheet often includes questions for family reflection during the days that follow. Some of our parallel assemblies that went particularly well include:

Finding God Every Day

Christian Models of Prayerful Living

Our Biblical Ancestors Show Us the Way

God's Call and Our Response

Living the Paschal Mystery

Reconciliation: Learn and Celebrate

The Word of God on Sunday and Every Day

Living Justly

Taste and See: The Importance of Beauty in Our Lives

Rediscover the True Meaning of Christmas

## INTERGENERATIONAL ASSEMBLIES

Intergenerational assemblies also begin with prayer, but then typically only very young children are taken to a special activity area (age three through kindergarten or grade one). Children and adults stay together, and the presentation usually includes activities that all can enjoy, and time for questions, dialogue, and/or faith sharing. Children enjoy the support of the adults who are present, while adults experience the presentation and activities through the eyes of the children. Each learns side by side with people of all ages. Some successful intergenerational assemblies include:

Vestments, Vessels, Symbols, and Signs (liturgical show and tell)

Hero Night (a night about saints and saintly living)

A Walk through the Mass

A Walk through the Sacraments of Initiation

A Walk through the Sacraments of Healing

It All Begins with Baptism

Light Our Way! (a celebration of Epiphany and the gifts we bring to share)

Living the Eucharist

Eating Our Way through the Gospels (potluck dinner and meal stories)

A Family Witness Night (witness talks by people of all ages in the context of prayer)

Weaving Our Way through the Liturgical Year (a brief presentation of the liturgical calendar, with stations that provide activities such as making an Advent wreath, a lenten calendar, a rosary, an alms box, etc.)

## ADULT FAITH FORMATION

Adult faith formation processes are richly varied, and most are the direct result of parishioner requests and feedback. Some include meals, others take on the structure of a "class." All include time for questions and dialogue among participants, and most also include time for social gathering. Popular sessions include:

Dinner for Married Couples

Discipleship Reflection (a one-day reflection on a spirituality of stewardship)

An Evening of Gifts Discernment

Men's Fellowship League (Monday Night MFL) (fellowship, speaker, sharing, followed by Monday night football on TV)

Grace-Full Women (music, fellowship, speaker on an aspect of women's spirituality, and table sharing)

Café Catholicism (coffee, light refreshments, and "hot topic" discussions)

Scripture Studies

Catechist Certification Courses (open to all who wish to attend)
  —Church History
  —Sacraments
  —Liturgy and Rites

Three-Part Series on Vatican II

Easter and Pentecost in the Scriptures

ASK: Adults Seeking Knowledge (akin to RCIA for Catholics)

Quench Your Thirst Days (question-driven dialogue)

Reading between the Wines

Senior Breakfast (Saturday morning following Mass, once each month. Breakfast and social time include a brief presentation by one of the pastoral staff, addressing topics of particular interest to senior members of the community.)

The Catholic Companion to *The Purpose Driven Life* (discussion with explanation of theological issues raised by a popular book).

## Combining Elements

Throughout the United States, parishes have begun choosing elements of whole community catechesis that address the needs of their specific communities. In some, classroom instruction for children is retained, but elements are added to expand faith formation to the whole community. Many parishes that keep classroom instruction have made a commitment to more meaningful catechesis in the following ways:

• Catechists or homeroom teachers are chosen because they have the gift of teaching, a gift of the Holy Spirit.

• Wide use of faith sharing at assemblies and within the classrooms helps children and adults integrate learning with life experience.

• Catechesis includes a connection to the Sunday assembly. Sunday readings are used for faith sharing.

• Liturgical catechesis is employed frequently and with much preparation and reflection.

Some parishes have moved away from classrooms and structured their assemblies to fulfill the same learning objectives as were met in classrooms, thus involving adults in instruction along with the children. A spiral scope and sequence is used so that everyone in the community may explore concepts in age-appropriate ways in the same period of time.

All gather and begin with prayer. At table, families reflect on the Question of the Week. Table leaders help facilitate discussion and connect the Question of the Week to the topic for the catechesis to follow. A large group presentation on the session's topic follows. Children may be sent to groups where they are catechized, using religion texts that follow a spiral scope and sequence. If children are sent to groups, adults participate in faith formation on the same theological concept as the children are exploring. The adult workshop invites participants to take the discussion home for further exploration.

In some parishes, catechesis happens at home or in neighborhood clusters. Families gather once each month to break open the Word. Following the faith sharing, a content driven presentation prepares families to use their religion texts at home during the month that follows. The evening ends with prayer, refreshments, and time for socializing. In between these monthly sessions, families meet at home or in clusters to study the lessons.

## SUMMER SESSIONS

In still other communities, catechesis for children who attend public elementary schools takes place in a two-week summer session. This summer catechesis is combined with assemblies throughout the school year and with adult faith formation to encourage lifelong conversion. (See the Appendix for a sample of the daily schedule for a summer session.)

Great flexibility is used in following this schedule. Sometimes middle school children spend one or more breakout periods with the youth minister. The pastor and other clergy visit for discussion or to answer questions.

Younger children sometimes take a tour of the church or take extra time to plan for the time they will lead prayer during the session.

A typical summer session day begins and ends with prayer. Each class takes a turn in leading prayer, which usually follows a modified morning prayer structure. The prayer begins with a song or with recorded music that is played as the assembly gathers. A psalm is sometimes sung, or at other times read antiphonally by the assembly. A brief passage of Scripture follows, and then the class provides a reflection on the Scripture through a skit or brief presentation. A song of praise, intercessions, or the Lord's Prayer and a closing song conclude the prayer.

Catechists begin preparation for the summer session by studying the archdiocesan graded course of study and by identifying concepts that are to be introduced, developed, or mastered at the grade level in which they will be teaching. Next, they go to the religion text for their grade level, and begin to study the text in light of the graded course of study. They identify sections of the text that are most important, and other sections that might require less instructional time. Then they begin to map out how they will cover the material in the time they have, often working with other catechists at their grade level to present information through a variety of approaches and always with the goal of connecting the information being given to everyday life. The catechists understand there are many opportunities for families to gather throughout the year, so they have freedom to concentrate on the concepts that have been specified for their grade level in the graded course of study.

# CHAPTER FIVE

# MEASURING SUCCESS

Will we be able to demonstrate that what we are doing is having any impact? That was one of the questions uppermost in my mind in winter 1997, as we administered the Assessment of Religious Education (ACRE) for the first time. (ACRE is now the Assessment of Catechesis/Religious Education.)

We were beginning registrations for the religious education students for the following school year, including, for the first time, a summer catechetical option in which parents make a commitment to continue family formation throughout the coming year. This would mean that much of our energy would be devoted to adult formation, as well as to running a summer session for children, while continuing the winter catechetical program and the Catholic education within our parish school of nearly 700 children. It would be a busy year, and I hoped that ACRE could help us identify areas that most needed attention. ACRE did help.

As we poured through reports that detailed our school and parish program children's understanding of concepts, our 1997 ACRE summary made it clear that there was much to be done. We were able to identify specific areas for catechists in both the parish school and Parish Religion Program (PRP) in which children were either confused or simply did not grasp concepts the catechists believed they had taught. Likewise, and equally important, we were able to identify areas of strength. Catechists in both programs were excited to find that their children did retain much of the information that was presented in religion sessions.

The beliefs/attitudes/practices/perceptions section (what I explain as the "lived faith" section) of the assessment was equally illuminating. We were able to pinpoint areas that could be reinforced in classes, enabling the students to apply better what they were learning to real life situations. We were provided with a window into the way our families integrated prayer and faith into their daily lives. We were even more convinced of the need for ongoing adult formation after studying the ACRE lived faith reports.

Our ACRE summaries were shared with our formation and education advisory commissions, and I began to detail the approaches we were putting into place to address what we were learning from ACRE, along with information from surveys given to families in our Parish Religion Program (PRP), evaluative material produced by the formation commission, and verbal input from adults in the community. By fall 1997, we had developed strategies to address the conceptual areas that demanded attention in both the school and PRP. We began designing adult and family formation opportunities, using the catechumenate and our "lived faith" section of ACRE as we determined topics for presentations and seasonal activities for families to do together throughout 1997-98.

What took place between our 1997 and 2000 administrations of ACRE was nothing short of wonderful. The adults who participated in the family formation evenings in 1997-98 were encouraging and grateful that they were being given an opportunity to learn and to grow along with their children. By spring 1998, we realized that the Wednesday evening PRP was on its way out, because only thirteen children were registered for the fall term.

At the same time, the summer program grew four times its original 118 children, expanding to two sessions of 200 each. Things were beginning to change rapidly, but we held fast to the areas we had identified as needing attention, based on all of the factors listed earlier.

Fall 1998 saw the addition of weekly evening prayer and adult formation on Wednesdays. Our pastor asked the parish staff to leave Wednesdays open for prayer and formation, and they have done so. Our public schools make every attempt to keep their calendars open on Wednesdays for local church activities, and the summer PRP parents were eager to help with family formation evenings that would take place on the first Wednesday of every month. The following spring we added faith formation on the Fridays in Lent, and our lenten series has added depth and variety to the formation opportunities available.

Four full seasons of faith formation at Immaculate Heart of Mary had led to a growing, thriving series of opportunities for children, youth, families, and adults.

I was eager to administer ACRE again, because my initial question was still with me. Could we actually demonstrate, in a standardized and measurable manner, that what we were doing was having an impact on those who participated? Our summer PRP catechists assured us that their children were retaining information from one year to the next and that they required less relearning than children in the winter program. Parents echoed the catechists' assessment, and added that their families were now able to attend Sunday Eucharist together. The formation evenings had given them opportunities to learn and to discuss their faith together. There was, however, this little voice in the back of my mind that wondered, "Is this working as well as it appears?"

The 2000 ACRE report summary arrived just before Easter and even a cursory glance provided startling insight. Yes, the summer PRP students were retaining what they were learning, much more markedly than their winter PRP counterparts, even when they took ACRE five months after they had completed their program. The school students improved dramatically in some of the areas we had ear-marked as needing special attention. There were areas in which the winter PRP students were responding with one hundred percent accuracy.

Most dramatic, however, were the "lived faith" sections of

the assessment. The families who had most faithfully attended the family formation evenings were the summer PRP families. The children in summer PRP demonstrated lived faith responses similar to those of the students in the school. Some of the summer PRP percentiles were higher. Most noticeable among those was the item that asked if the children always attend Sunday (Saturday evening) Mass.

While children in the winter program were near the national average of forty percent and the school children were a bit above at fifty-two percent, the summer PRP response was sixty-eight percent. We won't really be ecstatic until we have one hundred percent of our families attending Mass on a weekly basis. We believe, however, that now we are able to demonstrate in a standardized and measurable manner the impact of adult and family formation on the way our parishioners live their faith. Participation in Sunday Mass is essential to living as Catholic Christians. ACRE, verbal and written feedback from parishioners, and the discernment of our advisory commission, help us understand the impact of faith formation toward growth in discipleship.

The chart that follows illustrates the change in scores between the 1997 and 2000 administration of ACRE. We administered the new ACRE in 2002, and scores raised slightly in each section, with Mass attendance now being reported in each of our programs at sixty-five to seventy percent.

We now see an increase in the winter PRP scores, too. The increase can be attributed to two major factors: ongoing adult and family formation has now been consistently offered for seven years, and there is a cumulative effect for everyone in our community. Secondly, many more of the winter program catechists are now archdiocesan-certified as a result of the availability of catechist certification courses at the parish and because many of our winter catechists also wish to serve in the summer program (which requires that catechists be either certified teachers or certified catechists). The combination of better prepared catechists who possess the gift of teaching and the ongoing faith formation for adults and families is having a measurable impact on everyone in our community.

For more information on ACRE, contact:

NCEA/ACRE

National Catholic Education Association

1077 30th Street, NW

Washington, D.C. 2007-3852

www.ncea.org

# Comparison of ACRE Assessments

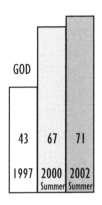

GOD

| 43 | 67 | 71 |
|---|---|---|
| 1997 | 2000 Summer | 2002 Summer |

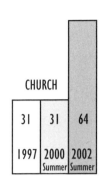

CHURCH

| 31 | 31 | 64 |
|---|---|---|
| 1997 | 2000 Summer | 2002 Summer |

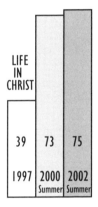

LIFE IN CHRIST

| 39 | 73 | 75 |
|---|---|---|
| 1997 | 2000 Summer | 2002 Summer |

REVELATION, SCRIPTURE, AND FAITH

| 31 | 57 | 68 |
|---|---|---|
| 1997 | 2000 Summer | 2002 Summer |

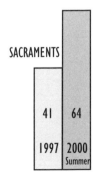

SACRAMENTS

| 41 | 64 |
|---|---|
| 1997 | 2000 Summer |

WORSHIP

| 31 | 31 |
|---|---|
| 1997 | 2000 Summer |

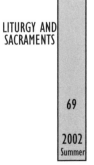

LITURGY AND SACRAMENTS

69

2002 Summer

PRAYER RELIGIOUS PRACTICES

69

2002 Summer

# APPENDIX

Gathering Song
*Choose a familiar hymn, ideally something that speaks of the Body of Christ or of bringing about the reign of God.*

| | |
|---|---|
| Leader | May the grace and peace of Christ be with us all. |
| All | Amen. |
| Leader | Let us begin our time together reflecting on God's Word. |
| Reader One | A reading from the Acts of the Apostles (Acts 2:42–27) |
| | They devoted themselves to the apostles' instruction and the communal life, to the breaking of bread and the prayers. A reverent fear overtook them all, for many wonders and signs were performed by the apostles. Those who believed share all things in common; they would sell their property and goods, dividing everything on the basis |

of each one's need. They went to the temple area together every day, while in their homes they broke bread. With exultant and sincere hearts they took their meals in common, praising God and winning the approval of all the people. Day by day the Lord added to their number those who were being saved. The Word of the Lord.

*Pause for silent reflection.*

Leader          Let us listen now to words from our bishops.

Reader Two      We seek to form parishes that are vitally alive in faith. These communities will provide a parish climate and an array of activities and resources designed to help adults more fully understand and live their faith. We seek to form adults who actively cultivate a lively baptismal and eucharistic spirituality with a powerful sense of mission and apostolate. Nourished by word, sacrament, and communal life, they will witness and share the Gospel in their homes, neighborhoods, places of work, and centers of culture. (From *Our Hearts Were Burning within Us*, page 5)

Leader          What words or phrases from these readings speak to you most powerfully? (pause)

What do these passages say about who we are as church? (pause) How might these passages influence our work at this meeting? (pause)

## FOCUS QUESTIONS

Now invite participants to move into small groups of four or five to consider the following: What are your dreams for our parish? Describe your vision to those in your group. If the people gathered are not familiar with the dimensions of whole community catechesis, the leader will need to briefly describe each dimension (as in chapter one). Following the descriptions, invite individuals to reflect on these dimensions and rate them (see below) in light of what is happening in the parish. On a scale of 1-5 (1=low, 5=high), rate your parish on each of these dimensions. Share with your group the reason for your ratings.

| | | | | | |
|---|---|---|---|---|---|
| The Eucharistic Liturgy Is Central | 1 | 2 | 3 | 4 | 5 |
| People Readily Share Their Faith | 1 | 2 | 3 | 4 | 5 |
| Parishioners Embrace Discipleship | 1 | 2 | 3 | 4 | 5 |
| Adults Are Actively Engaged | 1 | 2 | 3 | 4 | 5 |
| Catechesis Involves Everyone | 1 | 2 | 3 | 4 | 5 |
| The Catechumenate Is the Model | 1 | 2 | 3 | 4 | 5 |

| Parishioners Are Called Forth to Use Their Gifts | 1 | 2 | 3 | 4 | 5 |
|---|---|---|---|---|---|
| People Build Households of Faith | 1 | 2 | 3 | 4 | 5 |

After each person has an opportunity to share his or her ratings within the group, take a brief break.

The leader now takes a few moments to describe each element of whole community catechesis (as in chapter two). In small groups, discuss each element in relation to your parish community.

- Which elements are already in place?
- Which elements are most important to include as your parish embraces whole community catechesis?
- Which elements might be of benefit later?
- Is there someone you would invite to help implement one or more of the elements?

Ask each person to think silently about the following:

- By beginning on the path of whole community catechesis, I hope our parish will....

After people have had an opportunity to reflect quietly for a few moments, invite participants to share their hopes aloud, using a sung or spoken response after each person shares.

Conclude with the Lord's Prayer, a blessing, and a sign of peace.

# A Look at Current Parish Adult Faith Formation and Ideas for Future Planning

(Sample Chart for one of the six elements of Adult Faith Formation
from *Our Hearts Were Burning within Us*)

## Missionary Spirit
*(Living and Spreading the Good News)*

| LITURGY | FAMILY- OR HOME-BASED | SMALL GROUPS | LARGE GROUPS | INDIVIDUAL |
|---|---|---|---|---|
| Ministry of Hospitality | Small faith group discussions | Social ministries formation | Booster/team formation | Prayer |
| The Mass | Bulletin inserts | Soup kitchen, etc. | Vacation Bible School | Library resources |
| Occasional speaker at the end of Mass | Advent and outreach | Giving trees | After Mass socials | Apologetics: a tool for empowering evangelization |
| Hospitality Sunday displays and sign-ups | Ongoing mission activities | Just faith, voluntary simplicity, other formation experiences | Catholic men's and women's events | What about a missionary spirit "fair" with ways to develop understanding and/or involvement? |
| Ecumenical services | Guided family discussion groups | RCIA | Twin community activities (garage sale, etc.) | Living and spreading the Good News through example |

## Worksheets to Assess Current and Future Faith Formation Processes

Develop worksheets (like the one on the following page) with your advisory group to illustrate what is already taking place in your parish and where there are "holes" in your catechetical processes. Create one worksheet for each of the six elements of faith formation detailed in *Our Hearts Were Burning within Us*: Liturgical Life, Knowledge of the Faith, Missionary Spirit, Community Life, Prayer, and Moral Formation.

After studying *Our Hearts Were Burning within Us* with your advisory group, take time to complete the worksheet for each element of faith formation, listing the opportunities that already exist for people to be formed through the liturgy, in family or home-centered processes, in small groups, large groups, or as individuals. These charts enable you to visually represent catechesis that is currently offered, and you will also easily see the areas that are most in need of development.

Once you have completed a set of charts for adults, do the same for children and teens. Begin to think about what an adult who embraces ongoing conversion "looks like" in relationship to the six elements of faith formation; then trace opportunities for individuals beginning with their preschool years. How is the parish providing opportunities for growth in faith over the span of a lifetime?

# A Typical Year of Meetings

| | |
|---|---|
| August | Day of reflection that includes prayer, meditation, reflection, sharing, and a look at the whole picture of catechesis within the parish |
| September | Adult faith formation |
| October | Children and family formation |
| November | Youth formation |
| December | Social gathering and a pulse check: what does the whole picture look like at present? |
| January | Combined meeting with the Social Ministries Commission to consider catechesis in justice, mission, and service, or with the Stewardship Commission to develop a spirituality of stewardship within the parish |
| February | Sacramental preparation |
| March | Typically a month without a meeting (Lent) |
| April | Evaluation of the past year's processes |
| May | Recommendations for the next year; leave-taking for members who end their term |
| June | Information meeting for potential new members and discernment for officers for the coming year. We have a chairperson, a chair-person-elect, and a secretary. Members take turns developing the prayer reflection for the meetings and for bringing snacks. |

# SAMPLE DAILY SCHEDULE FOR A SUMMER SESSION

| | |
|---|---|
| 8:30—8:45 AM | Catechists and staff gather for prayer and preparation. |
| 9:00—9:15 AM | Opening prayer: Student-led, with adult support. Parents and younger siblings join when possible. |
| 9:15—10: 45 AM | Instructional block |
| 10:45—11:45 AM | Mini-session break-outs for art, music, youth ministry, snack, etc. |
| 11:45 AM—1:15 PM | Instructional block |
| 1:15—1:30 PM | Closing prayer: Student-led, with adult support. Parents and younger siblings join when possible. |

# SAMPLE PLANNING CALENDAR

## January

Light Our Way! Parish Celebration of Ministry

Movie Nights and Church History series begins

Grace-Full Women, season II begins

Women's Tea

Parent Evening on the Eucharist; Summer/Home Study reunion

**Preparation**

Lenten series preparation

Long range planning meetings

Lenten small group, material development

Hospitality Sunday (our first) preparations

VBS Team Meetings begin

## February

Senior Breakfast

Dinner for Married Couples

Grace-Full Women

Church History

Hospitality Sunday

Vatican II, short course

SFC, leaders pick up

Materials for lenten season

Rite of Welcoming

Jeremiah Retreat, middle school youth

Lenten series begins

**Preparation**

Quench Your Thirst Days, preparation

Lenten series, prep continues

PRP/YC Registration Packets prepared

Prep for Purification and Enlightenment

Long Range Plan Goal Proposals due

# SAMPLE PLANNING CALENDAR

## March

Lenten series, each Friday

Small faith communities meet

Rite of Election, Penitential Rite, Scrutinies, Presentations of Creed and Lord's Prayer

Purification and Enlightenment, evenings of reflection

First Reconciliation

Women's Christ Renews His Parish

Quench Your Thirst Days begins

**Preparation**

PRP/YC, registration begins

Easter Vigil preparation

Weekly prep for lenten series evenings

Early Summer PRP, preparation

Long Range Plan, parishioner prioritization gathering

Prep for A Night to Remember

Prep for "Jesus" (May)

## April

Quench Your Thirst Days concludes (April 1)

Final Catechumenate Minor Rites

Triduum

Celebration of Easter Vigil

First Eucharist Mini-Retreats

Confirmation

Begin new Grace-full Women series on prayer

Men's CRHP

**Preparation**

Evaluation of lenten series and gathering of ideas for 2005 (Formation Commission)

Final preparation for First Eucharist Celebrations

PRP/YC Registration

Summer PRP catechist preparation

Fall family formation, envisioning /speaker line-up

# Resources

## Whole Community Catechesis

Huebsch, Bill. *Whole Community Catechesis in Plain English.* Mystic, CT: Twenty-Third Publications, 2002.

————. *Handbook for Success in Whole Community Catechesis.* Mystic, CT: Twenty-Third Publications, 2004.

————. *The General Directory for Catechesis in Plain English.* Mystic, CT: Twenty-Third Publications, 2001.

Rotunno, Jo McClure. *Heritage of Faith: A Framework for Whole Community Catechesis.* Mystic, CT: Twenty-Third Publications, 2004.

## Liturgy/Sacrament

Hughes, Kathleen. *Saying Amen: A Mystagogy of Sacrament.* Chicago: Liturgy Training Publications, 1999, especially chapters 1 and 2.

Phillipart, David. *Saving Signs, Wondrous Words.* Chicago: Liturgy Training Publications, 1996.

Worship Office of the Archdiocese of Cincinnati. *We Gather in Christ: Our Identity as Assembly.* Chicago: Liturgy Training Publications, 1996, especially chapters 1, 2, and 6.

## Stewardship/Community/Parish Climate

Johnson, Elizabeth. *A Catholic Kid's Guide to Stewardship.* Mystic, CT: Twenty-Third Publications, 2004.

Hueckel, Sharon. *The Disciple as Steward.* Currently out of print, but available via Leisa Anslinger.

Liturgy Training Publications and Tabor Publishing. *A Common Sense for Parish Life.* Chicago: Liturgy Training Publications, 1995.

Rademacher, William J. with Rogers, Marliss. *The New Practical Guide for Parish Councils.* Mystic, CT: Twenty-Third Publications, 1995, especially chapters 7 and 8.

Articles Highlighting Planning, Implementation, and Impact of WCC at Immaculate Heart of Mary Parish, Cincinnati, OH

Anslinger, Leisa. "Demonstrating and Measuring Success in Religious Education." *Momentum,* February/March, 2002.

————. "Planning, Developing, and Evaluating Alternative Models of Catechesis." *Catechist,* April/May, 2003.

————. "Faith Formation with Families in Mind." *Momentum,* September/October, 2003.

Poust, Mary DeTurris. "Teaching Your Children Well." *Our Sunday Visitor,* August 24, 2003.

Shadle, Joe. "Getting Parents More Fully Involved." *Today's Parish,* January, 2003.

Retreat and Renewal Resources

Life in Christ Retreat: p. 50-77 *Handbook for Success in Whole Community Catechesis.*

Christ Renews His Parish Retreat: P.O. Box 19100, Cleveland, OH 44119, 216-731-7903

RENEW International: 1232 George Street, Plainfield, NJ 07062, 908-769-5400, Renew-intl.org